BULLETPOINTS

THE GREEKS
AND THE TROJAN WAR

MiLes
KeLLy
PUBLISHING

First published in 2004 by Miles Kelly Publishing Ltd
Bardfield Centre, Great Bardfield
Essex, CM7 4SL

Copyright © 2004 Miles Kelly Publishing Ltd

2 4 6 8 10 9 7 5 3 1

Editorial Director: Belinda Gallagher
Picture Research: Liberty Newton
Production: Estela Boulton

Designed and packaged by Q2A Creative

British Library Cataloguing-in-Publication Data
A catalogue record for this book is available from the British Library

ISBN 1-84236-494-4

Printed in China

www.mileskelly.net
info@mileskelly.net

The publishers would like to thank the following artists for contributing to this book:
Peter Dennis/Linda Rogers, Nicholas Forder, Luigi Galante, Alan Hancocks, Richard Hook,
John James, Roger Kent, Kevin Maddison, Janos Marffy, Alessandro Menchi, Chris Odgers,
Terry Riley, Mike White

The publishers would like to thank the following sources for the use of their photographs:
Page 25 Warner Bros.; (38) Warner Bros.; (39) Warner Bros.

All other images: MKP Archives; Dover; PhotoDisc

Contents

The glory of the Greek civilization

- **The ancient Greek civilization** began around 4000 years ago. It was one of the earliest civilizations of the world.

- **The ancient Greeks** lived in independent city-states or *polis*. The word politics is derived from *polis*.

- **The largest city-states** were Athens and Sparta. Others included Thebes and Corinth.

- **Each city-state** had its own laws, customs and traditions. However, all ancient Greeks spoke the same language and believed in the same gods.

- **Until 508BC**, the city-states were ruled by either oligarchs (a group of aristocrats) or tyrants (self-appointed rulers). But in 508BC, the world's first democratic government was created in Athens.

▶ *This two-handled amphora vase is a typical example of ancient Greek art. These vases were used to store wine and oil, and often depicted ancient Greek myths.*

. . . FASCINATING FACT . . .

Tyrants in ancient Greece were not always bad rulers. Most of the tyrants came from aristocratic families and seized power only when they felt that the existing government was unfair and ineffective.

- **The word democracy** is derived from the Greek terms *demos*, meaning people, and *kratos*, meaning rule. All citizens (except slaves and immigrants) had the right to vote in the Assembly that was held every ten days.

- **Greek men** took active interest in the running of the government and in matters of trade. Hence, they spent a lot of time away from home.

- **Women in ancient Greece** had limited freedom. They could go outside the home only on special occasions, such as marriages, funerals and religious festivals. But at home, the women were in full charge.

- **Slaves were vital** to ancient Greece. They worked in the fields, factories and mines, and had no rights. Even the names they used were given to them by their owners!

- **Most slaves** were prisoners of war. Some of them were children of slaves, while others were children who had been abandoned by their parents. Some poor families sold their members into slavery.

▶ *The ancient Greeks wore simple clothes. Men wore tunics made of wool or linen and woollen cloaks during winter. Women wore ankle-length dresses.*

Famous Greeks

- **Ancient Greeks** were great scholars. Their contributions to the fields of astronomy, geography, medicine and mathematics are invaluable.

- **Some of the more famous Greek** scholars include Socrates, Plato, Aristotle, Archimedes, Pythagoras and Hippocrates.

- **Socrates, Plato and Aristotle** were the three great men of philosophy. The word philosophy means 'love of wisdom'.

- **Socrates (466–399BC)** encouraged people to think about truth and life. However, Socrates never recorded any of his teachings. Most of what we know about him has been gathered from Plato's writings.

▲ *Hippocrates rejected the then existing theory that diseases were caused by the anger of the gods or by evil spirits.*

- **Plato (427–348BC)** was the disciple of Socrates. His famous works include the *Apology* and *The Republic*.

- **Aristotle (384–322BC)** studied at Plato's Academy. He was trained in medicine and had great knowledge of astronomy. He was the first to classify animals according to similarities in their characteristics.

- **Greek mathematicians** such as Euclid, Pythagoras and Archimedes are responsible for many of the basic formulae that are still used in algebra and geometry.

- **Hippocrates (460–377BC)** is considered to be the 'Father of Medicine'. He is the author of the famous Hippocratic Oath that talked about the patient's rights and explained a doctor's responsibilities towards his patient.

- **Herodotus (c 484–c 425BC)** is said to be the world's first historian. His most popular work, *Histories*, deals with the expansion of the Persian Empire and the Greco-Persian Wars.

- **Aesop's fables** are hot favourites among children, even today. The fables are still used to instil good morals in youngsters.

- **According to Herodotus**, Aesop was a slave in Samos. It is believed that after his master freed him, Aesop served in the court of King Croesus of Lydia.

◀ *Hipparchus, the Greek astronomer, is credited with calculating the length of a year and the distance between the Earth and the Moon.*

Entertainment

- **Ancient Greeks** loved music, dance and other forms of entertainment. In fact, they were one of the first civilizations to build a theatre.

- **The Greeks developed** several styles of play. They gave the world tragedies and comedies.

- **The word 'drama'** has been derived from the Greek word *dran* meaning 'to do' or 'to act'.

- **The Theatre of Dionysia** at Athens hosted an annual competition called the Great Dionysia. Playwrights from all parts of Greece participated in this event.

- **The three most renowned** authors of tragic plays were Aeschylus, Sophocles and Euripides.

- **Sophocles is believed** to have written over 100 plays, of which only seven are left. He is also said to have won the Great Dionysia festival over 20 times.

- **Aristophanes was the best** comic dramatist in ancient Greece. Through his play *The Cloud* and *The Frogs*, Aristophanes ridicules the philosophy of Socrates and Euripides.

- **Aeschylus was well-known** for writing a group of three plays based on the same theme. These are called the trilogies. The *Oresteia* is the only trilogy that survives.

- **Only Greek** men were allowed to act in plays. During the play the actors wore masks. Men wore wigs to enact the roles of women.

- **The main scene** was acted on a raised centre stage. Actors in the orchestra danced and sang during the play. These actors were called the chorus.

▼ *Plays in ancient Greece were usually performed in outdoor theatres such as this. But indoor theatres, called Odeia, also existed. The term theatre has been derived from the Greek word theatron meaning 'seeing place'.*

Games

- **The ancient Greeks** loved sports and they held several competitions to show off their physical strength. They also believed that the gods favoured strong men.

- **The competitions** (collectively called the Pan-Hellenic Games) included the Olympic, the Pythian, the Isthmian and the Nemean Games. Of these, the Olympic Games were the most popular.

- **The Olympic Games** were held every four years at Olympia in the honour of Zeus. All wars were stopped during the month the Games were held.

- **The first** Olympic Games are believed to have been held in 776BC. In AD394, the Games were banned by the Roman emperor, Theodosius.

- **Only those athletes** who had trained for at least ten months were allowed to participate in the Games.

- **The athletes participated** in a variety of events such as running, pentathlon, boxing, chariot racing and a foot race with armour.

- **Women**, slaves and foreigners were not allowed to participate in the Olympic Games. Women were not even allowed to watch, so they held games of their own called Heraea.

- **In the beginning** the winners of the Olympic Games were given olive branches. But as the Games grew popular, winners were also given prize money and other gifts.

- **In 1896**, Baron Pierre de Coubertin, a French educator and sports enthusiast, revived the Olympic Games. The first modern Olympics was held in Athens.

- **Women athletes** participated in the Games for the first time in 1900. From 1908, winners of the first three positions began to be awarded with medals.

▲ *If a man won the first three events of the Olympic Games the rest of the events were cancelled. The winners were presented with a pot of olive oil, with a picture of the sport the person competed in.*

···FASCINATING FACT···
Athletes in ancient Greece used to compete naked. In fact, the word gymnasium comes from the Greek word *gymnos*, meaning naked.

The Titans and the Olympians

- **The Titans**, also known as the elder gods, were a group of twelve immortals who ruled the earth before being overthrown by their descendants, the Olympians.

- **A prophecy claimed** that Cronus, the King of Titans, would be overthrown by his own son. So when his children were born, Cronus ate them.

- **When Zeus was born**, Cronus's wife, Rhea, was scared for him. She tricked Cronus into swallowing a rock, thus saving Zeus.

- **Zeus grew up** and poisoned Cronus, who vomited up all the children he had swallowed. They were Poseidon, Hades, Hera, Demeter and Hestia.

- **After fighting the Titans** for ten long years, Zeus, along with his brothers and sisters, finally overthrew the Titans with the help of the hundred-handed Giants and Cyclops.

▲ *Prometheus was born to the Titan Iapetus and his wife, Asia, the nymph. Prometheus had three brothers, Menoetius, Atlas and Epimetheus. The name Prometheus means 'foresight'.*

- **Zeus banished the Titans** to Tartarus in the underworld. He punished Atlas, who led the Titans, by making him hold the world on his back.

- **Prometheus, the wisest Titan**, who had fought with the Olympians, was spared. He created Man and gave him the gift of fire, much against the wishes of Zeus.

- **Prometheus continued** to defy Zeus and help mankind. Angered by his disrespect, Zeus had Prometheus chained to a rock on the Caucasus Mountain, where each day, a giant eagle devoured his liver, which kept renewing.

- **Years later**, the mighty Heracles, son of Zeus, killed the giant eagle to free Prometheus from his torment.

- **Prometheus returned** the favour by helping Heracles in one of his twelve labours. Prometheus guided Heracles to the garden of the Hesperides, where Heracles killed the dragon guarding the tree and obtained the golden apples.

▲ *His first labour required Heracles to kill a dreaded lion that lived in the hills around Nemea. Heracles choked the beast to death and wore its skin like a cloak.*

...FASCINATING FACT...
Goddess Hera, the wife of Zeus, hated Heracles. She drove Heracles mad and caused him to kill his family. Upon realizing what he had done, Heracles sought purification. The oracle of Delphi told him that he had to perform twelve labours in order to be purified.

The legendary heroes

- **Ancient Greek mythology** talks about several heroes. Apart from Heracles, who is the most popular, other Greek heroes included Jason, Theseus, Oedipus and Perseus.

- **Jason was the prince of Iolcus.** He was sent to Chiron the Centaur, when his uncle imprisoned his father and seized the throne.

- **When Jason returned** to Iolcus to claim his throne, his uncle challenged him to prove his worth by bringing back the legendary Golden Fleece.

- **Jason set off** on his quest along with a group of brave people, including Heracles. The group was called Argonauts after their ship, the *Argo*.

- **After surviving many perils**, Jason and the Argonauts returned victorious.

- **Perseus was the son of Zeus,** who with the help of Goddess Athena, killed Medusa, the snake-headed Gorgon.

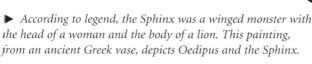

▶ *According to legend, the Sphinx was a winged monster with the head of a woman and the body of a lion. This painting, from an ancient Greek vase, depicts Oedipus and the Sphinx.*

- **Theseus was the son of King Aegeus.** When Theseus learnt that every year young men of Attica were sent as human sacrifices to King Minos of Crete, he set off on a mission to solve the problem.

- **At Crete**, Theseus was thrown into a labyrinth in the Palace of Knossos, where the young men were devoured by the Minotaur, the bull-headed son of King Minos's wife.

- **Theseus slew the monster** and escaped the labyrinth with the help of Ariadne, the daughter of King Minos.

- **Oedipus caused the death** of the terrible Sphinx that guarded the gates of Thebes. The Sphinx killed all those who could not answer her riddle. Until Oedipus came along, no one had succeeded in giving the correct answer.

▲ *Myth has it that the Minotaur was created when Poseidon, the sea god, made Minos's wife Pasiphae fall in love with a bull. Their affair resulted in a child with a human body and a bull's head.*

FASCINATING FACT

According to legend, the Golden Fleece was that of a ram belonging to Hermes, the messenger of gods. It was protected by a fierce dragon.

Homer and the epics

- **Homer is the ancient Greek poet** who is believed to have written the famous epic poems – the *Iliad* and the *Odyssey*.

- **Not much is known about Homer**. It is believed that he lived around 700BC in Ionia. It is thought that he was blind.

- **The *Iliad* deals with the Trojan War**. According to the poem, Paris, the Trojan prince, kidnapped Helen, wife of Menelaus, a Spartan king. Enraged by his actions the Greeks attacked Troy.

- **Even before his birth**, it was predicted that Paris would cause Troy's destruction. So, his father, King Priam, abandoned him on Mount Ida.

- **As destiny would have it**, Paris lived and the predictions came true. The *Iliad*, however, does not recount the story of Paris. In fact, the poem starts with the final year of the war.

- **The *Odyssey* tells the story of the** Greek hero, Odysseus. It deals with his journey back home, after the Trojan Wars.

▲ *Homer's work is considered to be a defining moment in Greek history. In fact, a lot of our knowledge about ancient Greece comes from his poems.*

- **According to the poem**, it took Odysseus ten years to return to Ithaca. On the way, he encountered several perils.

- **In one of his adventures** Odysseus blinded Polyphemus, the Cyclops, who ate some of his crew members.

- **Polyphemus** was the son of Poseidon, the sea god, who avenged his son by making Odysseus's journey more difficult.

- **Odysseus survived** all his adventures with the help of goddess Athena, his guardian. Upon arriving in Ithaca, Odysseus killed his wife's suitors to be reunited with his family.

▲ *Virgil, a well-known Roman poet, wrote the epic poem* Aeneid, *which told the story of Aeneas, the Trojan prince. Virgil's style was similar to that of Homer. In fact, he was called the 'Roman Homer'.*

···FASCINATING FACT···
After the Trojan War, Aeneas, the only Trojan prince to survive, travelled to Italy, where he founded Rome. It is believed that Augustus Caesar, the famous Roman emperor, was his descendant.

The Trojan War – how it began

- **The cause of the Trojan War** can be traced back to the marriage of Peleus and Thetis, a sea nymph. All gods except Eris, the goddess of discord, were invited to the wedding.

- **Eris was enraged** at this oversight and stormed into the party. In order to disrupt the ceremonies, Eris threw a golden apple on the table. The words *Kallisti*, meaning 'for the fairest', was inscribed on it.

▲ *Helen was the daughter of Zeus and Leda, wife of King Tyndareus of Sparta. This image depicts the temple of Zeus.*

- **The goddesses** began quarrelling over the apple. Zeus interrupted them saying that Paris, the most handsome man on Earth, should decide the winner.

- **The three goddesses** rushed to Paris and tried to bribe him. Hera offered him political power and Athena gave him the chance to become the greatest warrior ever.

- **Aphrodite offered Paris** the most beautiful woman on Earth, Helen. Paris promptly gave the apple to Aphrodite.

- **With Aphrodite's blessings**, Paris left for Sparta to kidnap Helen. Helen's husband, Menelaus, treated Paris like a royal guest.

- **When Menelaus left Sparta** to attend a funeral, Paris kidnapped Helen and also loaded his ship with a great deal of Menelaus's wealth.

- **Paris married Helen in Troy**. Menelaus was outraged that Paris had taken Helen. He called upon his brother and Helen's old suitors to help get her back.

- **Helen's beauty** had earned her many suitors. Odysseus, the King of Ithaca, was also one among them.

- **In order to avoid a fight** amongst the suitors, Odysseus made all the suitors swear that they would defend Helen's husband from anyone who posed a threat.

▼ *The statue of Athena in the Parthenon at Athens. Athena was unhappy that Paris chose Aphrodite over her. This led to Athena helping the Greeks during the Trojan War.*

War is declared!

- **Agamemnon, the King of Mycenae**, was the brother of Menelaus. He had married Helen's sister, Clytemnestra. Agamemnon was chosen to lead the Greeks in the war against Troy.

- **Many of Helen's old suitors** did not want to join the war. Odysseus pretended to be mad. But Palamedes, Prince of Euboea, uncovered Odysseus's secret, forcing him to ally with the Greeks.

- **Achilles was not** one of Helen's suitors. Yet, the Greeks needed him to fight because of a prediction that Troy would not be captured unless Achilles joined the war.

- **Achilles pretended** to be a woman to avoid fighting. However, Odysseus tricked Achilles into giving up his true identity.

- **Philoctetes**, son of King Poeas of Meliboea, also joined the Greeks. He was one of the Argonauts who went in quest of the Golden Fleece. He was also a close friend of the legendary Heracles.

- **On the way to Troy**, Philoctetes was bitten by a snake. Since his wound had a terrible smell, Odysseus left him stranded on the island of Lemnos.

The Lion Gate

- **When the Greeks landed** on the coast of Troy, they found Hector, Paris's brother, waiting for them with his army. Hector killed Protesilaus, the leader of Phylaceans, the moment he stepped off his ship.

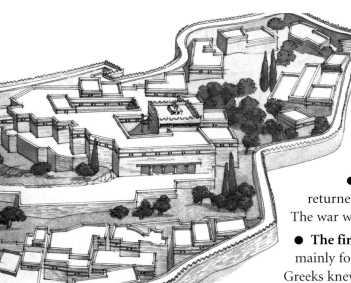

● **Even though** Hector had made clear his intentions to fight, the Greeks sent Menelaus and Odysseus to negotiate with King Priam. But the king refused to return Helen and the stolen treasure.

● **Menelaus and Odysseus** returned to their fleet, empty-handed. The war was now inevitable!

● **The first nine years** of the war were mainly fought against Troy's allies. The Greeks knew, that to weaken Troy, they had to first cut off her supplies.

▲ *Mycenae was amongst the strongest forces in the attack against Troy. The Lion Gate was one of the most important features of the Mycenaean citadel. It represented the city's power and prestige.*

.....FASCINATING FACT....
Odysseus pretended to be insane by ploughing his fields and sowing salt instead of seeds. The clever Palamedes put Odysseus's son, Telemachus, in front of his plough. Odysseus immediately steered the plough away, thus revealing his sanity.

And the war raged on

- **The Trojan War** continued into its tenth year. Agamemnon stole Briseis, who was Achilles' slave. Offended, Achilles withdrew his troops from the war.

- **Achilles' absence** weakened the Greeks and Hector was able to establish major victories. Achilles' friend Patroclus sought his permission to return to the battlefield.

- **Achilles allowed Patroclus** to fight and gave him his armour. Hector mistook Patroclus for Achilles and killed him.

- **Grief stricken**, Achilles returned to the battlefield to kill Hector and avenge the death of his dear friend.

- **It is believed** that when Achilles was an infant, his mother, dipped him in the river Styx to make him invincible. But she held him by the heel, leaving that part of his body vulnerable.

- **In the war**, Achilles defeated several Trojan allies. He helped the Greeks to gain the upper hand once again. Eventually Paris killed Achilles by shooting an arrow in his heel.

▶ *The story behind Achilles' mortality gave rise to the phrase 'Achilles' heel', which in the modern context refers to a person's weak point.*

● **After the death of Achilles**, Odysseus and Ajax fought for his armour. The shrewd Odysseus obtained the support of the rest of the Greeks. Having lost the contest, Ajax went mad and killed himself.

● **In the course of time**, the Greeks captured Helenus, son of King Priam and Cassandra's twin. The Greeks tortured Helenus, a prophet, into revealing the future.

● **Helenus predicted** that the Greeks could not win without Philoctetes, who had been given the bows and arrows of Heracles. Odysseus and Neoptolemus, Achilles' son, then persuaded Philoctetes to join them.

● **Machaon**, a healer from Thessaly, healed Philoctetes' wound. Philoctetes went on to kill many Trojan leaders, including Paris, with the divine bows and arrows of Heracles.

▲ *In one scene of the* Odyssey, *Odysseus's faithful dog Argus dies just as his master reaches his home town, Ithaca. After the Trojan War, it took Odysseus another ten years to finally arrive at Ithaca.*

. . . **FASCINATING FACT** . . .
The Greek fleet that went to retrieve Helen is believed to have consisted of a thousand ships. That is where the famous line 'the face that launched a thousand ships' came from.

The fall of Troy

- **The death of Paris** did not end the Trojan War. A prediction by Helenus said Troy was protected by the Palladium, a statue fallen from the heavens.

- **The Greeks were sure** that this prediction was true. The brave Odysseus disguised himself as a beggar and entered the city. Helen recognized him and helped him to steal the Palladium.

- **To conquer the Trojans**, the Greeks needed to enter Troy. Odysseus ordered a huge wooden horse to be built. The inside of the horse was hollow so that he and his soldiers could hide in it.

- **Epeius**, one of the Greek soldiers, built the horse according to the plan. He designed the structure with a hollow belly and an opening on one side. The horse was completed in just three days.

- **The Greeks** then led the Trojans to think that they were giving up the battle. They sent the Trojan Horse as a peace offering and pretended to leave the city.

- **Cassandra**, the daughter of King Priam of Troy, warned the Trojans that accepting the horse would lead to the destruction of Troy. Apollo, who was in love with her, had blessed her with the power to predict the future.

- **Cassandra could not love Apollo.** In anger, he put a curse on her that no one would ever believe what she said. She told the Trojans many times not to accept the Trojan Horse but nobody took her seriously.

> ...FASCINATING FACT...
> 'Trojan horse' has become a term for someone or something that undermines from within. For example in computers, it is commonly used to refer to any computer programme that disguises itself as a harmless application, enters a computer by deceit, and damages it.

- **The Greek spy Sinon** convinced the Trojans to accept the horse. The Trojans truly believed that the Greeks had given up. They accepted the 'gift' and took it into their city. Little did they know that an army of Greek soldiers were waiting within the hollow structure, ready to attack.

- **The Trojans celebrated** what they thought was a huge victory. When the hidden Greek soldiers emerged from the horse, they took the joyous people of Troy completely by surprise.

- **The Greek warriors** opened the city gates to let in the rest of their army. Troy was destroyed and the Trojan War ended in a bloody battle brought on by the Greeks.

▼ *Laocoon, a priest in Troy, also warned the Trojans about the horse. He even thrust a spear inside it to prove that there were people inside, but the Trojans did not listen to him. This scene of the Trojan Horse being taken into the city is from the movie,* Troy.

Divine interventions

- **The ancient Greek gods** played a vital role in the Trojan War. In fact, the war itself was the result of a contest between goddesses.

- **The gods Poseidon and Apollo** built the walls of Troy. When King Laomedon refused to reward them as promised, Poseidon vowed never to protect Troy from its enemies – he in fact helped the Greeks during the Trojan War.

- **Apollo**, on the other hand, sided with the Trojans. He was offended when Agamemnon abducted the daughter of Chryses, Apollo's priest. He sent a plague to the Greek camp to punish Agamemnon.

▲ *Poseidon turned against the Greeks following their misdeeds after the war. As a punishment, he stirred up storms to delay the return of the Greek heroes to their homelands.*

- **Apollo also saved** Aphrodite's son, Aeneas. Diomedes, the King of Argos, had injured Aeneas and would have killed him but for Apollo's intervention.

- **Before the Greek fleet** left for Troy, Artemis, the goddess of hunting, stopped the winds in Aulis, delaying the fleet's departure. She wanted to punish Agamemnon, who had boasted of being a better hunter than her.

- **In a bid to please Artemis**, Agamemnon sacrificed his daughter, Iphigenia. Agamemnon's wife, Clytemnestra was outraged by his actions and killed him on his return.

- **Hera and Athena** were angry with Paris for choosing Aphrodite over them. So, they stood by the Greeks. Athena even fought during the war.

- **Aphrodite and her lover Ares**, the god of war, protected the Trojans. At one time, Ares entered the fray in the guise of a warrior. Diomedes recognized him and warned his men to fall back.

- **Hera urged Diomedes** to throw his spear at Ares. Diomedes obeyed and Athena drove the spear into Ares' body. Wounded, Ares fled the battlefield and the Trojans fell back.

- **Zeus did not interfere** for the most part, until Thetis asked him to on behalf of Achilles. Hephaestus, the God of Fire, made Achilles' armour when he returned to the war after the death of Patroclus.

◄ *This is the temple of Artemis. Some believe that Artemis saved Iphigenia from being sacrificed by substituting her with a deer. It is said that she was then made a priestess of Artemis. Others consider Iphigenia to be another form of Artemis.*

27

Greco-Persian Wars
– the prelude

- **Around 560BC**, the Lydians, led by their King Croesus, conquered Ionia. Later, in 546BC, the Persians under Cyrus defeated the Lydians and took control of the area.

- **Around 499BC**, Aristagoras, the ruler of the Ionian city Miletus, encouraged the Ionians to revolt against the Persians. The Ionians managed to oust many of the Persian leaders and set up democracies.

- **Fearing retaliation** from the Persian Emperor, Darius, Aristagoras enlisted the help of mainland Greeks. Sparta refused to help. However, Athens extended her support.

- **The Ionian revolt** was, however, quelled. In 494BC, Darius defeated Aristagoras and recaptured Miletus. Athens's involvement in the conflict led to Darius invading Greece.

- **In 492BC**, Darius took on the Athenians at the battle of Marathon. The Athenians, with Plataea's support, scored a major victory.

- **According to a legend**, Pheidippides, a Greek messenger, ran from Marathon to Athens to convey the news of the victory. Soon after delivering the message, he died of exhaustion. The marathon race has its origin in this legend.

▶ *When the Olympic Games were revived in 1896, the marathon race was introduced to honour Pheidippides. The race covered the same route that Pheidippides took from Marathon to Athens. Spiridon Louis, a Greek athlete, won the race.*

- **To avenge the defeat of Darius**, his son, Xerxes invaded Greece in 480BC. He met the Greeks at the narrow pass at Thermopylae. This time, the Spartans and Corinthians had also entered the fray.

- **The Greeks set up barricades** to stop the Persians. For several days, both sides fought in a fierce battle. But the Persians could not penetrate the Greek defence.

- **After a few days**, a Greek traitor led a part of the Persian army in by another route. The Persians came from behind and surrounded the Greeks.

- **Leonidas, the Spartan general,** stayed back with some of his troops to keep the Persians at bay, while the rest of the Greek army escaped. Leonidas died fighting.

▲ *Darius I ruled Persia from 521BC until 486BC. After his death, his son, Xerxes ascended the throne. Although Darius managed to suppress the Ionian Revolt, he could never establish complete control over the Greeks.*

. . . FASCINATING FACT . . .
King Croesus was the first to mint gold and silver coins.
He is believed to have obtained his wealth from the legendary Midas,
the king who turned everything he touched into gold.

Triumph over Persia

- **After the battle of Thermopylae,** the Athenians fled to the island of Salamis. Meanwhile, the Persians, led by King Xerxes, destroyed Athens and Attica and continued to pursue their enemy.

- **By this time** the rest of the Greek fleet, including the Spartans, had joined the Athenians at Salamis. The Athenian commander, Themistocles, convinced his allies to stay at Salamis and fight the Persians at sea.

▼ *The Battle of Plataea was the last main battle between the Greeks and the Persians. But another 30 years passed before Athens and Persia finally signed a peace treaty.*

- **The Greeks** had over 350 triremes and *penteconters* (50-oared ships). Of these, around 180 belonged to Athens. The Persian fleet was much larger, with 1200 ships.

- **The Persians were confident** of defeating the enemy. Xerxes even set up a throne on the shore in order to watch the battle and identify the commanders who brought him glory.

- **The clever Themistocles** sent a slave named Sicinnus into the Persian camp. Sicinnus informed Xerxes that the Greeks had decided to retreat during the night, since they could not agree upon a location for the battle.

- **Xerxes believed** the slave and sent his fleet in search of the Greeks, who were in fact sleeping in their ships. The Persian fleet blocked the exit of the strait and searched for signs of retreat all night.

- **The next day** the tired Persians sailed into the strait and attacked the Greeks. A fierce battle followed. The big Persian ships could not move about easily in the narrow strait and were destroyed by the lighter Greek ships.

- **After the defeat**, Xerxes returned to Persia. But he left Mardonius behind to control the conquered areas. With the help of his small force, Mardonius managed to recapture Athens.

- **In 479BC**, the Greek city-states once again came together to fight the Persians at the final Battle of Plataea. Mardonius was killed in the battle and the Persians were forced to withdraw from Greece.

- **Following their victory** in the Persian Wars, the Ionian states formed the Delian League. The members of the league promised to protect each other from foreign attacks. Athens was made the head of the league because of her strong naval force.

The Peloponnesian War

- **Athens used** its powerful position in the Delian League to expand its territories. In 454BC, Pericles moved the Delian Treasury from the island of Delos to Athens.

- **Sparta and Corinth** hated Athens's supremacy. They saw Athens as a threat but were not ready to take her on in a war.

- **In 431BC**, Thebes attacked Plataea. Athens rushed to Plataea's defence. Sparta and Corinth joined Thebes – the war was on!

- **Two years passed**, neither side had made any gains. But then, a devastating plague struck Athens, killing thousands of people – Pericles was one among them!

- **Pericles's death** weakened Athens. The oligarchs wanted peace and eventually managed to negotiate a treaty with Sparta. However, the 30-year truce lasted only seven years.

▲ *At the age of 70, Socrates was brought to trial. He was accused of being an atheist and of corrupting the youth. The Athenian jury sentenced him to death.*

> ...FASCINATING FACT...
> Socrates, the famous Greek philosopher, was an Athenian soldier during the Peloponnesian War. He fought in the battles at Potidaea, Amphipolis and Delia.

- **In 415BC**, Alcibiades, Pericles's nephew, convinced the Athenians to attack Sicily in a bid to cut off supplies to both Sparta and Corinth.

- **Alcibiades** had just left for Sicily, when he was arrested on charges of destroying public statues. Outraged, Alcibiades escaped to Sparta, where he told the Spartans about the Athenian expedition.

- **Athens suffered** her worst defeat at Sicily but continued to put up a valiant fight. Alcibiades returned to Athens and led her to major victories, until he once again fell from favour.

- **In 405BC**, the last of the Athenian fleet was destroyed at the Aegospotami River. Athens never recovered from this loss.

- **In 404BC**, the Spartan army invaded Attica and forced Athens to surrender. Athens lost all her powers and became a subject of Sparta.

▶ *The Athenian fleet sent to Sicily consisted of over 100 triremes and around 27,000 soldiers. It was the largest fleet ever fielded by a city-state.*

33

Ancient Greek warfare

- **Greek warfare** in ancient times was very advanced and sophisticated. The military strategy of the Greeks was the main reason they succeeded against enemies like the mighty Persians.

- **The phalanx military formation** was a typical feature of the ancient Greek army. In this, each soldier was protected by the shield of the soldier next to him.

- **The Greek foot soldiers** were called hoplites. These hoplites were heavily armoured and carried ten-foot spears with iron tips. They also carried large bronze shields, which were effective in the phalanx formation.

- **The phalanx** was originally used by the Spartans. But it was Epaminondas, the Theban general, who developed it and put it to great effect.

▲ *The hoplites wore a bronze breastplate and protected their legs with bronze greaves. They also wore bronze helmets and carried short swords in addition to the spears.*

- **The phalanx usually consisted** of eight to sixteen rows of soldiers. However, Epaminondas opted for fifty rows against the Spartans at the Battle of Leuctra in 371BC. Needless to say the plan worked and Thebes scored a huge victory.

- **Around 367BC**, Philip II of Macedon was living in Thebes as a hostage. During this time, Philip learned about Greek politics and military strategies.

- **It is believed** that Philip gained much of his military knowledge from Epaminondas. He also studied the phalanx closely and identified its weaknesses.

- **In 359BC**, Philip ascended the throne and almost immediately embarked on his invasion of Greece. He created a military force on the lines of the Theban army particularly using the phalanx.

- **The Macedonian phalanx** was more advanced. Unlike its Greek counterpart, it could be manoeuvred easily. The hoplites also used a longer spear called *sarissa*.

- **Philip's son**, Alexander the Great, inherited his father's military genius. He too used the phalanx successfully in all his conquests.

▶ *The phalanx led the rest of the military in a battle. It pushed against the enemy phalanx until one broke the formation of the other, exposing its hoplites to certain death.*

The giant falls!

- **In 336BC**, King Philip was killed and Alexander the Great assumed the throne. Following in his father's footsteps, he launched an offensive against Persia.

- **Beginning with Asia Minor**, Alexander the Great gradually conquered Syria and Egypt within five years. He went on to defeat Darius III and become the ruler of the Persian Empire.

- **Alexander the Great** was not happy with just achieving what his father had dreamt of. After conquering Persia, he continued his march and invaded the East. He conquered Bactria and married a Bactrian princess.

▶ *Alexander the Great not only made Greece a great military power, but was also responsible for spreading Greek culture as far as the East.*

- **The greatest victory** for Alexander the Great came at the river Hydaspes (now called the Jhelum River). Here, he defeated Porus, the brave Indian king, in a fierce battle.

- **After conquering a large part** of the Indus River valley, Alexander the Great wanted to march on into the interiors of India. But his soldiers refused to go any further, forcing him to return to Babylon.

- **In 323BC**, Alexander the Great died. Since there was no one to succeed him, his vast empire fell into the hands of his generals.

- **The ambitious generals** started to fight amongst themselves. The son and brother of Alexander the Great died in this conflict of two decades.

- **By 300BC**, the empire of Alexander the Great had broken into four smaller empires. Asia Minor, Greece and Macedonia were ruled by Antigonus, while Egypt came under Ptolemy I, who started the Ptolemid Dynasty.

- **Seleucus**, who was a general in King Philip's army, crowned himself the king of Mesopotamia and the Middle East. All the four empires continued warring between themselves.

- **While the conflict** amongst the Greek empires grew, another power was slowly gaining importance. After regaining control over the Greeks in Southern Italy, the Romans went on to invade Greece.

> ...FASCINATING FACT...
> Cleopatra, the last pharaoh of Egypt, was not an Egyptian.
> She was a Macedonian Greek and a descendant of Ptolemy I,
> Alexander's general.

Recreating Troy

- ***Troy*** the movie stars Brad Pitt as Achilles, Eric Bana as Hector, Orlando Bloom as Paris, and Peter O'Toole as King Priam. Diane Kruger is Helen and Brian Cox plays Agamemnon, while Brendan Gleeson enacts King Menelaus.

- ***Troy*** was meant to cost $150 million to produce. However, it became one of the most expensive movies ever made. Production delays raised the budget to over $200 million.

- **Due to the war** in Iraq, the production of *Troy* was shifted from Morocco to Mexico in February 2003.

- **Brad Pitt trained** for six months to get into shape for his role as Achilles. His trainer was Duffy Gaver, who also helped actor Toby Maguire to build up his muscles for *Spiderman*.

- **Diane Kruger** was on a diet of pizzas and protein shakes to gain weight for her role. In ancient Greece, being curvaceous was a symbol of wealth.

- **Ironically**, Brad Pitt actually injured his Achilles' tendon while filming.

- **More than 1500** battle-trained extras were used in the film.

- **In Greek mythology**, Agamemnon survives the war and returns home, where his wife kills him. In the movie, Agamemnon is killed during the war.

▶ *In the recent film adaptation,* Troy, *Brad Pitt brings Achilles back to life.*

▲ *Only two fully functional ships were built for the movie. The remaining ships of the Greek fleet were rendered digitally. The two real ships were made of steel and clad in wood.*

- **Both Pitt and Bana** performed their own fight scenes for the film. They also made a pact, according to which they would pay a fine whenever they accidentally hit one another.

- **The fine** for light blows was $50, while harder blows resulted in a fine of $100. Brad Pitt apparently had to pay Eric Bana $750.

Index